Illinois
Facts and Symbols

by Emily McAuliffe

Consultant:
Richard A. Capriola
Special Assistant to the Superintendent
Illinois State Board of Education

Capstone press
Mankato, Minnesota

Capstone Press
151 Good Counsel Drive, P.O. Box 669, Mankato, Minnesota 56002
http://www.capstone-press.com

Library of Congress Cataloging-in-Publication Data
McAuliffe, Emily.
  Illinois facts and symbols/by Emily McAuliffe.—Rev. and updated ed.
  p. cm.—(The states and their symbols)
  Includes bibliographical references (p. 23) and index.
  Summary: Presents information about the state of Illinois, its nickname, motto, and emblems.
  ISBN 0-7368-2243-7 (hardcover)
  1. Emblems, State—Illinois—Juvenile literature. [1. Emblems, State—Illinois.
2. Illinois.] I. Title. II. Series: McAuliffe, Emily. The States and their symbols.
CR203.I3M38 2003
977.3—dc21   2002154791

Editorial Credits

Christianne C. Jones, update editor; Rebecca Glaser, editor; Kim Covert, additional editing; Linda Clavel, update cover designer; Clay Schotzko/Icon productions, cover designers; Kelly Garvin, update photo researcher; Michelle L. Norstad, photo researcher

Photo Credits

Index Stock Imagery/Mark Gibson, cover
James P. Rowan, 22 (middle)
Lynn M. Stone, 20
One Mile Up, Inc., 8, 10 (inset)
Richard Hamilton Simth, 6, 12
Root Resources/Ruth A. Smith, 14; Pat Wadecki, 16; Alan G. Nelson, 18
Unicorn Stock Photos/Dennis MacDonald, 10, 22 (top); Richard B. Dippold, 22 (bottom)

1 2 3 4 5 6 08 07 06 05 04 03

Table of Contents

Fast Facts about Illinois

Capital: The capital of Illinois is Springfield.

Largest City: Chicago is the largest city in Illinois. Nearly 3 million people live in Chicago.

Size: Illinois covers 57,918 square miles (150,008 square kilometers). It is the 25th largest state.

Location: Illinois is near the middle of the United States. It is bordered by Wisconsin, Iowa, Missouri, Kentucky, and Indiana.

Population: 12,419,293 people live in Illinois (2000 U.S. Census Bureau).

Statehood: Illinois became the 21st state on December 3, 1818.

Natural Resources: Illinois has coal, oil, clay, sand, and gravel.

Manufactured Goods: Illinoisans make farm machinery, foods, and electronics.

Crops: Illinois farmers grow soybeans, corn, wheat, and apples.

State Name and Nickname

The name Illinois comes from the Native American word Illini (i-LINE-eye). Illini was the name of a Native American tribe. The tribe lived in the area that is now Illinois. Illini means man. Illinois is the French spelling of the word.

People call Illinois the Land of Lincoln. Illinois has this nickname because President Abraham Lincoln lived there. Lincoln was the 16th president of the United States. He lived in Illinois before he became president. Springfield has many historic sites honoring Lincoln. One of the sites is a monument where he is buried.

Another nickname for Illinois is the Prairie State. A prairie is a large area of flat grassland. Most of the land in Illinois is flat. People also call Illinois the Corn State. Farmers grow corn on the Illinois prairie.

This monument in Springfield honors Abraham Lincoln.

State Seal and Motto

The state seal is a symbol. A symbol is an object that reminds people of something else. For example, the U.S. flag reminds people of the United States.

The state seal is a small picture pressed into wax. Government officials stamp the seal onto important papers. The seal makes government papers official.

The Illinois state seal shows a bald eagle. The bald eagle stands for the United States. The seal also shows a rock. The two dates on the rock are 1818 and 1868. Illinois became a state in 1818. The state adopted its seal in 1868. The stars and stripes stand for the first 13 states. The date August 26, 1818, appears around the seal. Illinois adopted its state constitution on this date. A constitution is a system of laws.

The Illinois state motto is State Sovereignty, National Union. A motto is a word or saying. Sovereignty means independence. The state motto means that Illinois is an independent state. But it is also proud to be part of the nation.

Illinois adopted this state seal in 1868.

State Capitol and Flag

Springfield is the capital of Illinois. A capital is the city where government is based.

The capitol building is in Springfield. Government officials work at the capitol. Some officials make laws for the state. Others make sure the laws are carried out.

The building is the state's sixth capitol. Workers began building it in 1868. They worked for 20 years. The capitol cost more than four million dollars to build.

The Illinois government adopted the state flag in 1915. The flag is white. The state seal appears in the middle of the flag. The state's name also appears on the flag.

The state name was not always part of the flag. An Illinois soldier noticed that many state flags looked alike. The soldier suggested adding the state name to the Illinois flag. The Illinois government added the name in 1970.

The capitol is in Springfield.

State Bird

The cardinal is the state bird of Illinois. Illinois students chose the cardinal in 1929. The cardinal is also the state bird of six other states. But Illinois was the first state to choose the cardinal.

Cardinals are easy to spot. Male cardinals are bright red. They have black markings around their beaks. Females are light brown with some red coloring. Both have red crests on their heads. A crest is a crown of feathers.

Cardinals' nests are shaped like a cup. They build their nests in bushes or shrubs. Cardinals eat sunflower seeds, grains, and wild berries.

Many birds travel to warm places in the winter. Cardinals do not. Cardinals stay in one area all year.

Male cardinals are bright red.

State Tree

The white oak is the state tree of Illinois. Students voted for the native oak in 1908. But there are many kinds of native oak in Illinois.

In 1973, students voted again. They chose the white oak as the state tree. White oaks grow in every Illinois county.

White oaks grow about 100 feet (30 meters) tall. Their branches spread out like an umbrella. Their bark is gray-white. Acorns are white oak seeds. Deer, wild turkeys, small birds, and squirrels eat acorns.

White oak wood is very strong. Furniture makers and ship builders use white oak. They know the wood will last a long time.

The U.S.S. *Constitution* is a famous sailing ship. It was built with white oak almost 200 years ago. The ship is still floating.

White oaks grow in every Illinois county.

State Flower

The native violet is the state flower of Illinois. Students chose the native violet in 1907. The Illinois government made it the state flower in 1908.

Native violets grow wild in many places. These small flowers grow in open prairies or lawns. They also grow in shaded woods.

Violet is a blue-purple color. But violets are not always purple. They can be blue, white, yellow, or red-purple. They usually have five petals on each flower. Petals are the colored outer parts of flowers.

Violets are food for animals and people. Mice and birds eat violet seeds. Rabbits eat whole violet plants. Some people make jelly from the flowers. Cooks decorate cakes with violet petals dipped in sugar.

Violets grow wild in Illinois.

State Animal

The white-tailed deer is the state animal of Illinois. Illinois students chose it in 1980. White-tailed deer are common. They live all over North America.

White-tailed deer are red-brown or gray. They have white on their chests and stomachs. White-tailed deer have bushy white tails. They raise their tails when they are afraid. This warns other deer of danger.

Young deer are called fawns. Fawns are spotted. They lose their spots when they are a few months old. Fawns are often born in June.

White-tailed deer eat grass, bark, twigs, and leaves. They also eat flowers and vegetables from people's gardens. They often look for food when the sun is setting.

Male deer grow horns called antlers. Their antlers fall off each winter. Healthy deer grow new antlers each year.

The white-tailed deer is the state animal of Illinois.

More State Symbols

State Insect: The monarch butterfly became the state insect in 1975. An insect is a small animal with a hard outer shell. Insects have six legs. Some insects have wings. The monarch has orange wings with dark spots.

State Fish: The bluegill became the state fish in 1987. The fish is named for the male's bright blue gills.

State Mineral: Fluorite has been the state mineral since 1965. People use fluorite to make steel, aluminum, and glass.

State Prairie Grass: The big bluestem became the state prairie grass in 1989. It is the tallest prairie grass in Illinois.

State Song: "Illinois" became the state song in 1925. Charles Chamberlain wrote the song. The song tells about the prairies, trees, and rivers in Illinois.

The monarch butterfly is the state insect of Illinois.

Places to Visit

Lincoln Home

The Lincoln Home is in Springfield. Abraham Lincoln lived in Springfield before he became president. The only home he ever owned is still there. The Lincoln family lived in the home from 1844 until 1861. Visitors can tour the brown two-story house.

Lincoln Park Zoo

The Lincoln Park Zoo is the oldest zoo in the nation. It opened in 1868. The zoo is home to more than 700 animals. Visitors can see elephants there. Visitors can also see gorillas in the Great Ape House. The Lincoln Park Zoo is open 365 days a year.

Shawnee National Forest

The Shawnee National Forest is in southern Illinois. It covers more than 260,000 acres (104,000 hectares). There are hills, lakes, and unusual rock shapes in the forest. Many kinds of wildlife live there. Visitors can hike, swim, camp, and fish in the forest.

Words to Know

capital (kap-UH-tuhl)—the city where government is based
crest (KREST)—a crown of feathers on a bird's head
insect (IN-sekt)—a small animal with a hard outer shell; it has six legs and sometimes has wings.
motto (MOT-oh)—a word or saying
prairie (PRAIR-ee)—a large area of flat grassland
sovereignty (SOV-ruhn-tee)—independence
state seal (SEEL)—a small picture pressed into wax; the seal makes government papers official.
symbol (SIM-buhl)—an object that reminds people of something else

Read More

Heinrichs, Ann. *Illinois.* This Land is Your Land. Minneapolis, Minn.: Compass Point Books, 2002.

Krummer, Patricia K. *Illinois.* One Nation. Mankato, Minn.: Capstone Press, 2003.

Santella, Andrew. *Uniquely Illinois.* State Studies. Chicago: Heinemann Library, 2002.

Sievert, Terri. *Illinois.* Land of Liberty. Mankato, Minn.: Capstone Press, 2003.

Useful Addresses

Illinois Department of Commerce and Community Affairs
Bureau of Tourism
620 East Adams
Springfield, IL 62701

Secretary of State: Chicago Office
69 West Washington
Suite 1240
Chicago, IL 60602

Internet Sites

Do you want to find out more about Illinois?
Let FactHound, our fact-finding hound dog, do the research for you.

Here's how:
1) Visit **http://www.facthound.com**
2) Type in the **BOOK ID** number:
   0736822437
3) Click on **FETCH IT**.

FactHound will fetch Internet sites picked by our editors just for you!

Index